BIBLE HEROES
& BAD GUYS

Other *2:52 Soul Gear* Books

Non-fiction
Bible Wars & Weapons
Weird & Gross Bible Stuff
Bible Fortresses, Temples & Tombs

Fiction
Laptop 1/Reality Shift
Laptop 2/Double Take
Laptop 3/Explosive Secrets
Laptop 4/Power Play

BIBLE HEROES & BAD GUYS

WRITTEN BY
RICK**OSBORNE**
MARNIE**WOODING**
ED**STRAUSS**

ILLUSTRATED BY
JACK**SNIDER**

Zonder**kidz**

Zonder**kidz**™

The children's group of Zondervan

www.zonderkidz.com

Bible Heroes & Bad Guys
Copyright © 2002 by Rick Osborne
Illustrations Copyright © 2002 by Jack Snider

Requests for information should be addressed to:
Grand Rapids, Michigan 49530

ISBN: 0-310-70322-0

Editor: Gwen Ellis
Art direction and design: Michelle Lenger

Printed in United States
02 03 04 05/RRD/5 4 3 2 1

CONTENTS

INTRODUCTION

It isn't always easy being a heroic kind of guy. You know the guy who tries to do things God's way. Someone who knows what God thinks is important and goes for it totally. Someone God and others can count on all the time!

Are you a heroic guy? Okay, okay that's a tough question because being God's kind of guy doesn't happen overnight. And maybe you're working on it, but you aren't there yet. Don't sweat it. God is willing and able to teach you how to be the kind of person that everybody wants around in a tight spot. It's kind of like learning to snowboard or doing the coolest ever back flip off the HIGH diving board. It takes a while, but stay with it and you finally get it.

God can help you grab hold of some pretty important tools for growing yourself into a hero. They're more powerful and more useful than any power tool you can handle. How about:

- Faith
- Trust
- Kindness
- Mercy
- Honesty
- Wisdom and
- Lots of courage.

**WAIT TILL YOU SEE THEM IN ACTION!
THEY REALLY WORK!**

God's got some awesome challenges for you to tackle in the future. But no problem! He'll get you ready for all your future heroic adventures if you're willing and ready.

Okay, then start with the Training Manual—the Bible. Inside the Bible are all kinds of important stories about guys doing the same thing you are doing today–learning to do it right. They, too, wanted to learn to be heroes, wanted to count for God, and refused to quit!

They did this by becoming:

- SMARTER
- STRONGER
- DEEPER in God and
- COOLER

It wasn't any easier for Bible guys than it is for you. No way! In fact, they didn't always make the right choices. But they wanted to please God. They were willing to do what he wanted them to do. And that made them total heroes! Some of these guys were:

- Joshua—master spy and warrior
- King David—giant slayer
- Paul—world traveler and big time survivor (And that was a long time before the TV show.)

BAD GUYS

Not only were there heroes in the Bible, but there were also some really bad guys who made some really bad choices. They didn't care about God or anyone or anything else. They didn't want to change their evil ways, lend a hand to anyone, or make the world a better place. Their lives were all about themselves. God had to deal with such guys as:

- Goliath
- Ahab
- Pontius Pilate

The important thing to remember is that heroes learn and villains burn.

So are you ready to go exploring into the past and see what kinds of people we can find in the Bible and what we can learn from them? Are you ready for your hero lessons? We can be sure we will be learning important lessons on what TO do and what NOT to do in our own lives. So let's climb into the driver's seat on the right road to becoming standup heroes and stay away from attitudes and actions of bad guy zero's.

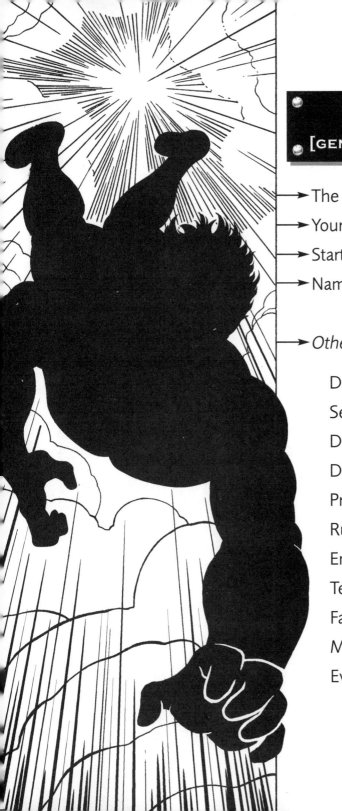

SATAN
[GENESIS—REVELATION]

→ The most awful, bad guy ever.

→ Your worst nightmare!

→ Started as an angel in heaven.

→ Named Lucifer.

→ *Other names for Satan:*

Devil

Serpent

Dragon

Destroyer

Prince of Demons

Ruler of Darkness

Enemy

Tempter

Father of Lies

Murderer

Evil One

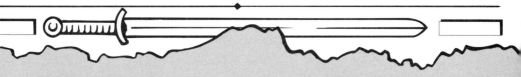

BAD NEWS

We don't know exactly what Satan [whom God had created and named Lucifer] did in Heaven. We do know he was powerful, good looking, and one of God's hotshot angels. We do know he rebelled (sort of like went to war) against God. Satan got a big-time attitude of PRIDE that led to a big-time battle in heaven. Basically Satan thought he was the ultimate best there was. He started thinking that God's chair was a place he could share. Wrong! Satan got a crash course in not messing around with God. He was thrown out of heaven and that was the beginning of sin on earth. God threw out other angels who were also rebellious. They were turned into demons.

Satan didn't quit after he was thrown out of heaven. He's

still against God, and still trying every way he can to control all of creation. He tricked Adam and Eve into sinning and he's still tricking us. Satan is BAD NEWS!

Good News

Satan is not as powerful as God. Not EVEN close! Satan is nothing more than a created being who chose to sin!

God knows everything ...
Satan only knows what he's learned.

God's everywhere at once ...
Satan can only be one place at a time.

God is all-powerful ...
Satan's power was reduced to zip when Jesus rose from the dead.

God IS in complete control of everything all the time ...
Satan can only be in control in our lives when we do things his way.

GET SMARTER

So you can see why Satan loves to get us away from doing God's will. Why would anyone listen to him? He's going to end up in an eternal lake of burning sulfur—you know that rotten-egg-smelling stink? Simple! Satan's very good at badly twisting the truth. We can get smarter by:

1) Remembering God is stronger than Satan and he's helping us.
2) Remembering God wins in the end and we can win, too, because God is more powerful than Satan.
3) Watch out for pride. If you are tempted to think you are better than someone else—STOP it!
4) And START to thank God for everything he has given you.

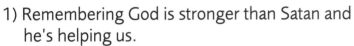

BIBLE SUPERCHARGE

When pride comes, shame follows. But wisdom comes to those who are not proud.

Proverbs 11:2

NOAH
[GENESIS 6:5—9:28]

A good man in a bad neighborhood.

Noah was a God-fearing, God-loving man.

He was listening when God told him to build an ark.

He was the father of three sons—Shem, Ham, and Japheth who started the human race over after the flood.

He stayed with the project until it was done.

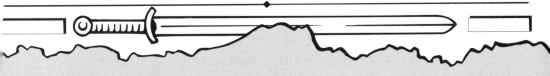
BAD NEWS

People were rotten in the time of Noah. Ever since Adam and Eve first listened to Satan, the world had become a hot spot for sin. God knew that when sin and Satan came along, people's hearts leaned to the dark side. God needed to let EVERYONE know that sin leads to a dead end. God decided to do a big demonstration with a one-time, hard-to-forget, world-wide flood. It was a wakeup call for everyone who would ever live.

So God told Noah to build a big ship (an ark). God said to make it 450 feet long, 75 feet wide, and 45 feet tall. It had windows, decks, and separate areas for the different kinds of animals. This was one humongous construction job, but Noah got it done.

His neighbors probably thought he was one oar short

of a working rowboat. But when he finished and the animals came to the boat, his neighbors knew he'd been telling the truth. After the door on the ark was shut, it started to rain and it kept on raining for 40 days and 40 nights. It rained and rained until the entire earth was flooded and all the bad guys were sunk.

Good News

Noah's floating zoo drifted for a long time—several months—and then sort of beached on top of Mount Ararat. God promised Noah and all living things that he would never again destroy the world with a flood and confirmed his promise with a rainbow. Noah and his family made sure the lesson that sin brings only bad stuff and punishment was passed on so everybody in the future would remember.

GET DEEPER

Even if everyone else is going his or her own way in the world today, we can still go the right way and be God's heroes. If God reached out and tapped you on the shoulder for a big, important job like Noah had, would you be listening? Would you know what he wants? Who knows, the entire planet could depend on your knowing and hearing God.

Something to think about!

BIBLE SUPERCHARGE

The Lord watches over the lives of those who are godly.

Psalm 1:6

ABRAHAM
[GENESIS 11:27-22-19]

Abram started out as a regular kind of guy.

God picked him for a special relationship and had regular conversations with him.

Abram believed when God said he would give him a new land.

After a while he got a new land and a new name—Abraham (Father of Many Nations).

GOOD NEWS

One day God told Abram to pack up his wife, servants, and all his sheep, cattle, and camels and move to a new land God would show him. That new land was going to be home for all his descendents from that time on. And God was going to make Abram rich. So even though he had no idea where he was going, Abraham went, and sure enough, God showed him the new land and gave him great wealth. And oh yes, God even gave him a new name—Father of Many Nations—or Abraham for short.

BAD NEWS

Now to be a father, you have to have kids, But Abraham and his wife, Sarah, didn't have kids. So how was he supposed to be the father of many nations. Then, when Abraham was 100 and Sarah was 90 along came their son, Isaac. Boy were Sarah and Abraham proud of that kid!

AND NOW SOME GOOD NEWS

Well, one day out of the blue, God asked Abraham to sacrifice Isaac on an altar. It was a test to see if Abraham trusted God. He was just about to sacrifice

Isaac when God stopped him. The test was over and Abraham passed.

Then Isaac grew up and had two sons. One of those sons, Jacob had twelve sons who had many sons and daughters and so on. They were Abraham's grandchildren. Now it looks like the father of many nations might actually get to be that. In fact, Abraham has millions and millions of blood relations on earth today.

One of Abraham's descendents was Jesus. Everyone who believes in Jesus can call Abraham the "father of his/her faith."

GET DEEPER

Abraham wasn't perfect and sometimes made mistakes, but for the most part he followed God's instructions. That's obedience! He believed God could and would do what he promised and would take care of him. That's trust! And God blessed Abraham. That's love! If we will do things God's way, and trust him to take care of us and our future, he will.

God loves us!

BIBLE SUPERCHARGE

Trust in the Lord and do good. Then you will live in the land and enjoy its food.

Proverbs 37:3

JOSEPH
[GENESIS 37– 50]

The eleventh son of Jacob.

Hated by his brothers.

Sold into slavery.

Imprisoned, falsely accused, and forgotten.

Became second in command in Egypt.

Saved a nation from starvation. Forgave his evil brothers.

AN OVERNIGHT SUCCESS?

Overnight success? Well sort of. His overnight success began when he was about seventeen. His brothers were very jealous of him and they sold him into slavery. They let their dad believe Joseph was dead. Hey, what are brothers for?

Joseph was taken to Egypt where he worked hard as a slave for the rich and powerful ruler of the land, Pharaoh. Pharaoh, the boss man, got to feeling he couldn't get along without Joseph! Then, just about the time things were going really great ... tough break. Joseph was thrown in jail on false charges.

Much later through a series of really strange happenings and dreams, Joseph was taken right back to the palace to tell Pharaoh what his dreams meant, and on the spot Pharaoh promoted him from prisoner to ruler.

JOSEPH SAVES EGYPT

Joseph's job was to pull together a fourteen-year plan to save the most powerful kingdom in the ancient world from starvation. Joseph couldn't believe what had happened to him. Only a few hours earlier he had been in jail on the long-term plan. One minute you're taking orders from the guards in cellblock zero and

the next you're telling Pharaoh how to run the kingdom! But when God said, "Okay, Joe, let's go," Joseph was ready and willing to step in. Through good and bad times, he trusted God. He saved the world from starvation. Eventually he was reunited with his family and saved their lives, too.

It's easy for us to look back at Joe's life and see God's plan. But it probably wasn't so easy for him when he was slogging it out as a slave or when he was sitting in jail singing the blues. But all the time God had a plan and was getting him ready.

GET COOLER

God has a plan for our lives too. We need to get ready by learning to trust God, applying ourselves to learning, growing, and doing our best no matter what life throws at us. We also need to be listening and to be ready when God needs a hero. It's good to remember that it might take years of learning and growing before God calls us into action.

BIBLE SUPERCHARGE

The sluggard craves and gets nothing, but the desires of the diligent are fully satisfied.

Proverbs 13:4

MOSES
[EXODUS 1–20]

- Born a Hebrew slave.

- Raised and educated as an Egyptian prince.

- Heard God from a burning bush.

- Got the Ten Commandments from God.

- Led the people out of Egypt. Wrote the first five books of the Bible.

- Talked face to face with God. Was a humble guy.

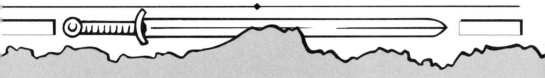
MISSION POSSIBLE

Moses. He's the guy who went toe to toe and hairy eyeball to hairy eyeball with the most powerful king on earth. Yet he was one of the most humble men who ever lived! Humble and great don't seem to go together, do they?

One day, God, speaking out of a burning bush, told Moses to go set his people free. Humble Moses didn't think he was the man for the job. But God gave Moses a pep talk and shoved him out the door (well actually back down the mountain). So Moses went off to tangle with Pharaoh.

After a whole bunch of miracles— like walking-sticks turned into slithering snakes, a hand covered in an instant with a creepy scab-peeling, withering mega-disease, and finally ten disgusting plagues of things like blood,

bugs, stinking pus boils, and death to your firstborn, Pharaoh decided to let Moses lead millions of Israelite slaves out of Egypt.

Moses marched them right down to the Red Sea and then with God's help he parted the water and helped his people escape to freedom in the wilderness. Moses led his people through danger after danger for 40 years.

MOSES GETS THE LAW

God had other jobs for Moses to do. He gave Moses the Ten Commandments or laws and then told him to teach the people how to live God's way. Moses also wrote the first five books of the Bible. Was Moses up to the tasks God gave him? Well, yes and no. On his own Moses' probably didn't have either the ability or the confidence to do the job. But with God as his partner, humble Moses knew God was doing all the hard things with him.

GET STRONGER

Moses had a hundred and one excuses why he wasn't the man for the job God needed done. But God wasn't buying it. God knew Moses was the right one because he was humble. So what is humble? Well:

- It isn't putting ourselves down.
- It isn't trying to do hard tasks.
- It is knowing that God will help you when you say YES to his plan.
- It is knowing you and God are partners.
- It is being confident that God knows what you can do with his help.

BIBLE SUPERCHARGE

So do not fear, for I am with you; do not be dismayed, for I am your God. I will strengthen you and help you.

Isaiah 41:10

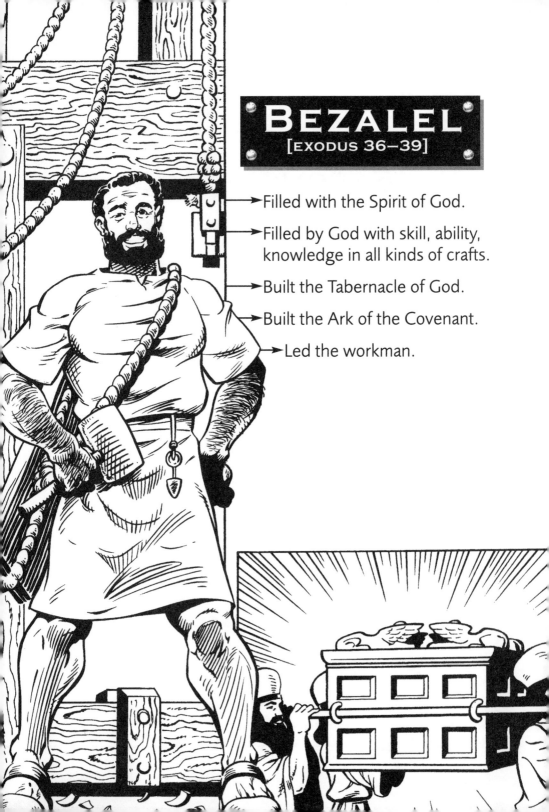

BEZALEL
[EXODUS 36–39]

Filled with the Spirit of God.

Filled by God with skill, ability, knowledge in all kinds of crafts.

Built the Tabernacle of God.

Built the Ark of the Covenant.

Led the workman.

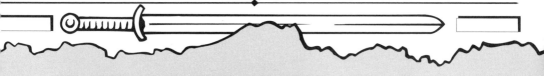
HE WAS THE ULTIMATE TOOL MAN

For 40 years the Israelites traveled in the wilderness. God wanted Moses and his people to have a place to worship him even when they were on the move.
So God instructed all the men and women to donate gold, silver, bronze, jewelry, yarn, cloth, animal skins, wood, spices, and olive oil for an awesome project.

Then God instructed a man named Bezalel to make something spectacular. It would be around for a long time and eventually would disappear.

SOME CLUES

1. It was God's throne room on earth.
2. It was made of gold and was incredibly beautifully.
3. It was phenomenally powerful and could kill men in an instant if they even looked inside it.
4. The Israelites took it into battle with them.
5. When captured, it brought horrible sickness and death to their enemies.
6. It is still one of earth's most puzzling mysteries.

God showed Bezalel how to manage the money and the people to build this treasure. "The Lord has filled him with the Spirit of God, with skill, ability, and knowledge in all kinds of crafts" (Exodus 35:31). Can you guess what it was?

PROJECT #1

Bezalel and the workers built a very cool-looking mobile temple (tabernacle). It could be taken apart and carried anywhere the Israelites went. It was 15 feet tall and 45 feet long. Inside the tabernacle candlelight reflected off all the gold that was there. This place was filled with God's presence and unlimited power! No matter where the tent was pitched that became the holiest spot on earth.

PROJECT #2

The most important project Bezalel did (and the one all the clues above are about) was a special holy chest called "The Ark of the Covenant." God showed him how to do it. The Ark of the Covenant was made out of carved wood overlaid with gold. Inside this box Moses put the Ten Commandments, Aaron's staff that Moses had used to do God's miracles, and a pot of manna. The Ark was so holy that if an ordinary person just touched it he or she would instantly die. It was so powerful that when the Philistines captured it, their cities were struck down by a terrible plague until they returned it to the Hebrews. When Bezalel's team had finished the tabernacle and all its furniture, the presence of the Lord filled it. God was very pleased with the talented, obedient, and original tool man—Bezalel. God had given him special talent. So Bezalel worked hard at getting very good at his talent. He was also willing to let God's Spirit work through him, so God could guide him.

GET SMARTER

God has lots of projects that need to be done. He'd like to use us, so we better work hard to develop our talents. We also need to listen for what he says to us. You can be sure God will keep our phone numbers handy for important jobs to be done.

BIBLE SUPERCHARGE

Do you see a man skilled in his work? He will serve before kings. He will not serve before obscure men.

Proverbs 22:29

BALAAM
[NUMBERS 22-31]

- Saw visions and heard from God.
- Dumber than his donkey.
- Didn't understand God's NO.
- Gave bad advice causing Israel to sin.
- Displeased God.
- Whimpered for mercy and God spared him.

Donkey
- Smarter than Balaam.
- Saw an angel blocking the road.
- Spoke outloud to Balaam and asked why he was beating him.

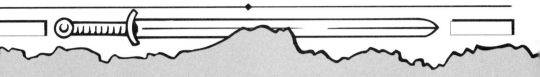

BAD IDEA

Balak, King of Moab, asked Balaam to curse the Israelites (his enemies). He would give Balaam a palace full of gold and silver to deliver the curse. Balaam asked God about the curse idea and God said, "You must not put a curse on those people, because they are blessed." In other words, God said, "NO."

End of story?
Not hardly.

Same song, second verse. Balak asked again. Balaam asked God again. God said no again. But this time an angel showed up to drive home the point (the angel had a deadly battle sword and it was drawn). Balaam didn't see the angel—but his donkey did. The donkey stopped and wouldn't go any farther. Smart donkey. Balaam beat

the donkey. Then the donkey spoke and asked Balaam why he kept beating him.

WORSE IDEA

Even after the conversation with the donkey, Balaam still didn't get it. Now he decided to advise the Midianites (friends of King Balak) to make friends with Israel, and then lure them into doing evil things. He hoped God would get so disgusted with the Israelites, he would curse them himself.

ENOUGH ALREADY

Balaam's plan worked—too well. Soon the people were worshiping idols and doing evil stuff. God told Moses to kill all the sinful leaders and toss their bodies out in the open so everybody would see them. God also sent a plague that killed 21,000 Israelites

After that the Israelites got the message, got smart, got right with God, and stayed right with God, God stopped the plague. The Israelites won the war against the Midianites. And Balaam got hacked down in the battle and died.

GET DEEPER

God has reasons for his yes's and no's. Doing an end run around him to get the solution you want is a bad idea. A good idea is to do it God's way and be obedient.

BIBLE SUPERCHARGE

Many are the plans of a man's heart, but it is the Lord's purpose that prevails.

Proverbs 19:21

JOSHUA
[BOOK OF JOSHUA]

- Learned well from Moses.
- Honored God.
- A true leader of men.
- A great warrior.
- Trusted God even when he was outnumbered.
- Knew that his victories came from God.

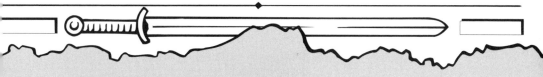

JOSHUA IN CHARGE

When Moses died, Joshua became the leader of Israel. He took a mob of ex-slaves and shepherds, gave them some leftover Egyptian weapons, and trained them into an elite fighting force that scared the professional armies of the land.

If Joshua was ever scared, he didn't show it. He believed God when God said, "No one will be able to stand up against you as long as you live. I will be with you, just as I was with Moses. I will never leave you. I will never desert you. Be strong and brave." After that pep talk, Joshua was ready for anything.

JOSHUA THE VICTOR

The first city Joshua attacked was Jericho. God had a strange plan for taking this city. March around it for seven days, then shout and the walls

would fall down. Joshua followed God's plan exactly and the walls fell down flat.

It happened again and again as Joshua followed God's plans precisely. Making sure the people did things exactly God's way was part of Joshua's job.

TWO MIGHTY MIRACLES GOD DID FOR JOSHUA WERE:

1. Stopped the sun in the sky so the Israelites could finish their battle with the Canaanites.
2. Rained hailstones that dented the heads of Joshua's enemies.

GET STRONGER

Joshua, with God's help, beat incredible odds and did the impossible. You can, too, and here's how:

1. Do things God's way.
2. Work smarter, harder, and do everything with all your might.
3. Pray. Ask God to help you and then trust him to do the impossible.

BIBLE SUPERCHARGE

Humility and fear of the Lord bring wealth and honor and life.
Proverbs 22:4

DEBORAH
[JUDGES 4–5]

→ A wife.

→ God's prophetess.

→ A leader of Israel.

→ A powerful judge.

SOME KIND OF WOMAN!

Deborah was kind of like the Moses of her time. She tried to make the Israelites stay right with God. She also kept her eye on their powerful, yet completely creepy neighbor, Jabin, king of the Canaanites.

King Jabin ordered his general, Sisera, to pull together a totally terminator army. Sisera got together 900 iron war chariots. (They were like the tanks of that day.) The soldiers were packing iron weapons as well.

Deborah had a serious conference with her commander, Barak. [Different guy from the one in the talking donkey story.] She told him to gather 10,000 tough guys for a big fight. Then God told Deborah how to win the battle.

Barak wasn't so sure they could beat the super-strong Canaanite army, and he said to her, "If you go with me, I will go; but if you don't go with me, I won't go."

"Very well," Deborah said, "I will go with you. But because of the way you are going about this, the honor will not be yours, for the Lord will hand Sisera over to a woman" (Judges 4:8–9).

Some Kind of Battle!

Next thing you know, Barak and 10,000 men noisily set up their tents on a mountain. That got Sisera's attention. He gathered his army in the flat plains (that's where his iron chariots could race around and cause the most damage) beside the Kishon River.

When Deborah shouted, "Attack!" Barak and his men swooped down the mountain. And just as they did (talk about timing!) God sent a rainstorm and a flash flood. The river overflowed its banks turning the plain into a swamp. Sisera's heavy iron chariots bogged down in the mud. What a sight! What a battle!

Chariots crashed to a stop and piled up all over the place like Saturday night at the demolition derby! Sisera and his men abandoned the fight and ran for home.

Sisera Meets Jael

Sopping wet and muddy, General Sisera hid in the tent of a woman named Jael. She took him into her tent, gave him milk to drink, and hid him. When he fell asleep, his happy hostess gave him a splitting headache by placing a tent peg to his head and pounding it straight through his brain and into the ground! When Barak ran by Jael's tent, she flagged him down and showed him the body. So a woman did defeat the great Sisera! With God's help, Deborah was the hero of the day.

GET COOLER

Deborah trusted God and was willing to send an army into what looked like a death trap. Talk about nerves of steel! Sometimes what we need to do will be tough. It may even look hopeless. But when we get into the action, God will join forces with us and what we do will make a huge difference! Yeah, and it helps to have godly friends stand with us.

BIBLE SUPERCHARGE

Be dressed ready for service.

Luke 12:35

SAMSON
[JUDGES 13–16]

→ Strong man.

→ Very brave.

→ Long hair.

→ Didn't drink wine.

→ Hated the Philistines.

→ Killed a thousand Philistines with the jawbone of a donkey.

→ Ripped off the city gates and took them to a mountaintop.

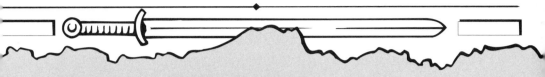
A Headstrong Hero

The Israelites cried out to God to help them crush the Philistines! God gave them a kind of ancient Superman—Samson. Samson's strength and power came from God. An angel told Sam's mom that he would be a very special kid and she had to raise him God's way. And oh yeah ... he could never get a hair-cut as a sign that he had been set apart by God for a very special job.

Real soon Samson learned to hate the Philistines. One day he was so angry with them that he tied torches to 300 foxes' tails and set them loose in the Philistines' wheat fields. Talk about toasted wheat! That did it! The Philistines were out to get him. One day they managed to tie him up with new thick ropes. But Samson wasn't the type of guy to hold still for THAT! He snapped them like string!

One Puny Little Weakness

The frustrated Philistines discovered Samson had one weak spot. What else? (Sigh!) Women. So the Philistines paid a woman named Delilah twenty-eight pounds of silver to find out what made Samson soooo incredibly strong.

Delilah sweet-talked that big, brawny lovesick guy into telling her that it was his uncut hair that made him powerful. Result? One night the Philistines secretly gave him a buzz-cut he'd never forget. His hair was gone and his strength was gone! The Philistines captured him, poked his eyes out, put him in chains, and made him grind grain in prison.

SAMSON COMES TO A CONCLUSION

One day the Philistine rulers brought Samson from jail to entertain their 3,000 guests. He'd been in jail a while and his hair had grown back and so had his strength. Samson prayed that God would give him super strength just one last time. Then he pushed on two main pillars of the temple and collapsed the entire roof! "Thus he killed many more [Philistines] when he died than while he lived" (Judges 16:30).

GET STRONGER

You know, maybe Samson started thinking he was the GREAT one, and that HE was the source of all his bulky power. Guys, take a tip from Samson's notebook. God is the one who helped Samson do great things in his life and God is the one who will help us do great things in our lives. So when you succeed at something, give God the thanks and credit for your success.

BIBLE SUPERCHARGE

Let not the wise man boast of his wisdom or the strong man boast of his strength ... but let him who boasts boast about this: that he understands and knows me, that I am the Lord.

Jeremiah 9:23–24

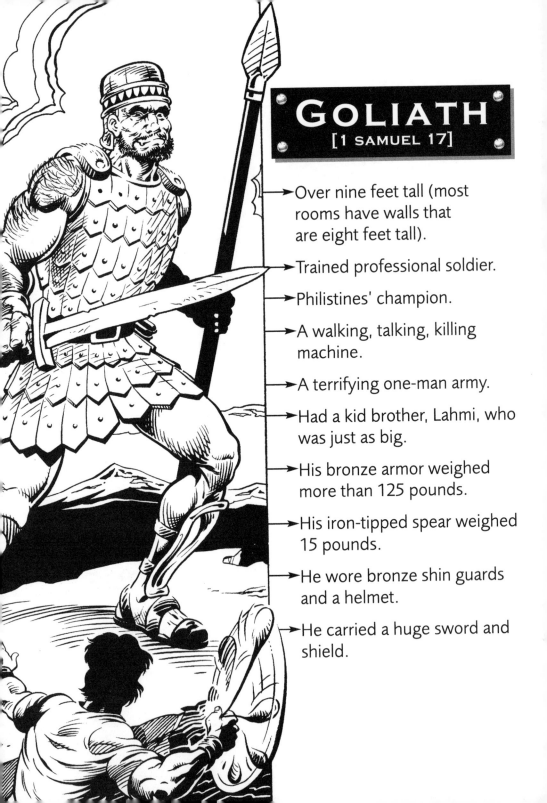

GOLIATH
[1 SAMUEL 17]

- Over nine feet tall (most rooms have walls that are eight feet tall).
- Trained professional soldier.
- Philistines' champion.
- A walking, talking, killing machine.
- A terrifying one-man army.
- Had a kid brother, Lahmi, who was just as big.
- His bronze armor weighed more than 125 pounds.
- His iron-tipped spear weighed 15 pounds.
- He wore bronze shin guards and a helmet.
- He carried a huge sword and shield.

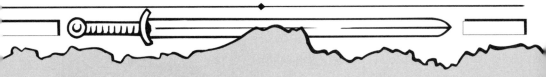
BAD NEWS

The first time Goliath stepped out onto the battlefield, the Israelites stared in disbelief. What a monster! Where'd the Philistines find this guy? The ancient world wrestling federation?

Each day Goliath would shout at the Israelite soldiers, "Why do you come out and line up for battle? Am I not a Philistine, and are you not the servants of Saul?

Choose a man and have him come down to me. If he is able to fight and kill me, we will become your subjects; but if I overcome him and kill him, you will become our subjects and serve us" (1 Samuel 17:8–9).

GOOD NEWS

One day a teenaged David wandered up to the frontlines, heard Goliath boasting and said, "Who is this ... Philistine?" (1 Samuel 17:26). With the king's okay, David gathered up his gear: a shepherd's staff, five smooth stones, and his sling and went to fight the giant. Goliath couldn't believe it! Israel's BEST warrior was a punk kid with a buzzard-chasing sling?

David, pumped up with adrenaline, sunk a stone into

Goliath's forehead and the giant did a face-plant in the ground. Then David seized Goliath's own sword and hacked off his head. In the custom of his day, David kept all of Goliath's fancy weapons and later took his head back with him to Jerusalem. (That's one disgusting souvenir.)

After a stunned moment, the Philistine army realized that a knobby-kneed kid had just done in their monster champion. The war was over! Last Philistine home was a rotten Israelite slave!

GET STRONGER

David had something (or Someone) on his side that Goliath didn't have! If we want to win the war against evil, we have to remember God is with us and that those who are fighting against God cannot win, big as they are. We also have to learn to trust God to help us use the talents he has given us in the right way. Just like David.

BIBLE SUPERCHARGE

Do your best to present yourself to God as one approved, a workman who does not need to be ashamed.

2 Timothy 2:15

DAVID
[1 SAMUEL 24]

- Youngest of eight brothers.
- Fought and killed a lion and a bear.
- Fought Goliath and won.
- Chosen to be king rather than Saul.
- God's guy—a man after God's heart.
- Mighty warrior who won all his battles.
- The greatest king Israel ever had.

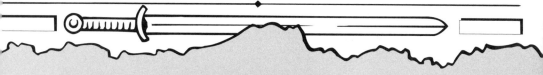
JUST AN ORDINARY KID

David was a tough little scrapper even as a kid. He guarded his father's sheep and even fought lions and bears. But during those lazy days watching sheep, David developed a very close and loving relationship with God. Then one day Samuel, the famous prophet, came walking into David's village and anointed him to be the next king. From then on, God began doing amazing things with David.

DEALING WITH THE BIG GUYS

David started his public career with a one-on-one victory over nine-footer, Goliath. The guy was practically packing a flagpole for a spear! But with a common ordinary rock from his sling, David had the guy dead out.

After beating the Philistine, David went to live in King Saul's palace. Soon everyone knew he was a young man going places. And then, whammo! David suddenly went from battle hero to royal enemy number one. King Saul was jealous of David and sent him to fight the Philistines just hoping that David would be killed. Sorry Saul, David killed 200 Philistines instead. More victory. More fame. More for Saul to be jealous about. And that's the way it stayed. David won all his battles. But now Saul knew David was God's choice for king and wanted him D-E-A-D. David went into hiding but the king was hot on his trail to murder him. David and his men hid out until King Saul died.

DAVID'S TURN

David did a lot of things as king. Some of them are:

- He made Jerusalem his capital.
- He brought the Ark of the Covenant there to stay.
- He created a strong army.
- With God's help, he totally creamed the Philistines.
- He also wrote most of the Psalms in the Bible.
- He ruled for 40 years.
- He died quietly in his sleep in his own palace.
- He was buried in Jerusalem—the city of David.

IF YOU FALL, GET UP AND START AGAIN

David really loved God, but sometimes he made some baaad choices. The thing about David was that every time he sinned, he humbled himself, begged for forgiveness, and got right with God again. David knew God loved him.

GET SMARTER

David always walked with God. And he learned from his mistakes. David didn't suddenly become great . It was a long process that started way back when he was a kid.

Same with us.

God starts training us for our big challenges and jobs from day one. We learn as we grow. So pay attention to the things you learn at church, home, school, sports field, or wherever! You probably won't be a king, but you just might use that training for an important job.

BIBLE SUPERCHARGE

Your hands made me and formed me; give me understanding to learn your commands.

Psalm 119:73

JOAB
[2 SAMUEL 18]

- King David's nephew.
- Commander of David's troops.
- He got jealous.
- He acted outside the rules.
- He didn't care if what he did was wrong.
- On a fast-track to power.

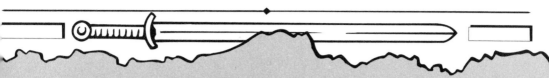

FOLLOW YOUR LEADER

Joab started his career by leading David's troops in a fight to see who would rule Israel—David or Saul's son Ish-bosheth. Abner was leading Ish-bosheth's army. David won and became king of all Israel.

Then Abner tried to come over to David's side so he could become one of David's generals. Wellll! That didn't go over so well with Joab. He wanted to keep his position as commander all to himself. So he decided to settle an old feud at the same time. He arranged a private "friendly" talk with Abner, then put a dagger in his guts and killed him.

This put Joab on David's black list. How could he get back on David's good list? Well, the Jebusites came to town. David said that whoever crawled up the water shaft into the city would be the new commander of the troops. Joab was up that shaft as fast as a rat up a drainpipe. David kept his promise, and Joab stayed on as army commander. But David didn't trust Joab completely and gave him only one-third of the troops.

FOLLOW THE INSTRUCTIONS OR PAY THE CONSEQUENCES

Before one big battle, King David ordered his men not to hurt his son. But during the battle, Absalom was riding his mule through a forest when he got stuck in a tree, caught by his hair. Joab found out and shoved not one, but three, javelins through Absalom's heart. Later cold-hearted Joab couldn't understand why David was so upset. "What's the biggie? It wasn't like Absalom was a good son."

That did it. David named Amasa as his right-hand guy. Joab didn't take that lying down. One day when both men were on their way to battle, Joab hugged Amasa. Only trouble was, he had a knife in his hand. He shoved it in and spilled Amasa's guts all over. That was the second time for that dirty trick.

Joab knew for sure now he was on the outs, so when another of David's sons, Adonijah, tried to steal the throne, not-so-loyal Joab joined him. Right about then David announced that his other son, Solomon, would be the next king. Oops! David advised Solomon to get rid of Joab and sure enough, when Solomon became king, he had Joab executed.

GET COOLER

Joab only loved people when they agreed with him or were useful to him. If anyone crossed him—watch out! We all like to win, but we can't do it by doing awful things to others—like tripping or pushing someone on the other team, before he can score.

Harsh words or mean actions should be off limits to us. We just have to leave tons of room in our hearts to love and pray for people who disagree with us. We need to have mercy toward those who mistreat us. Today's enemy might become tomorrow's best friend!

BIBLE SUPERCHARGE

There is a way that seems right to a man, but in the end it leads to death.

Proverbs 14:12

ELIJAH
[1 KINGS 17]

→ Called fire out of heaven.

→ Fed the widow and her sons.

→ Taught faith.

→ Was fed by a bird.

→ Did tons of miracles.

→ Went to heaven in a chariot of fire

→ Was a tough man of God.

→ Never died!.

BAD NEWS

One bad king after another had encouraged God's people to worship idols. God was extremely angry and sent Elijah to warn King Ahab to get right or start sucking back glasses of sand. You heard that right. God decided to send a drought and famine. He would turn off the rain for a few years to punish the kingdom of Israel for worshiping idols.

Well, when that thirsty (and bloodthirsty) king heard that, Elijah had to run for his life. God kept him safe by sending him to live far away with a widow and her son. God gave them food and water all during the drought. One day the woman's son died. End of story. No way! Elijah prayed and (Wow! Stand back!) God brought the boy back to life!

WATCH OUT FOR JEZEBEL!

Meanwhile King Ahab's wife, Jezebel, went into a screeching rage against God for sending the drought. To get revenge, she killed every prophet of God she could get her wicked, little painted nails on.

Want a fight, Jezebel? You got it. Showdown time. God told Elijah to call a massive meeting with the people of Israel. In this corne ... Elijah! In the other corner

... Jezebel's 450 prophets of Baal and 400 prophets of Asherah. Elijah explained the rules: Both groups would make an offering to their god. The god who answered by sending fire down was the one and only god.

For hours, the Baal boys prayed, shouted, danced, and slashed themselves with knives. Nothing happened. Elijah joked that they should shout louder in case their god was in bed, sleeping.

THE FIERY PROPHET

Then Elijah prayed to God. To the complete dismay of the Baal boys, "the fire of the Lord fell" (1 Kings 18:38). The people of Israel instantly shouted that God was the one true God. They didn't waste any time. They rounded up the priests of the idols, dragged them down the mountain, and slaughtered them.

When Elijah had finished his job as a prophet, God sent fire one more time. This time horses of fire pulled a chariot of fire, and a whirlwind whisked Elijah right up to heaven.

GET DEEPER

Fighting evil and making smokies out of your enemies can be a lonely job. Elijah was one guy against an evil world, and it made him feel very sad and alone, just like we feel when we are the only Christian kid at school. Cheer up! We're not alone! When you feel that kind of alone, remember that God gave us a church so we could connect with other Christians. So call and talk to a friend from church. And remember—God is nearby. He never wants you to feel alone.

BIBLE SUPERCHARGE

You are the body of Christ, and each one of you is a part of it.

1 Corinthians 12:27

AHAB
[1 KINGS 21]

- Winner of "The Most Evil King" award.
- Worshiped idols.
- Married an evil woman, Jezebel.
- Killed a man for his vineyard.
- Died in battle.
- Dogs licked up his blood.
- Ruled 22 years.

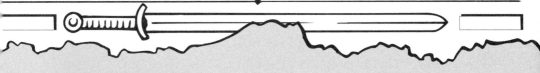

BAD NEWS

Ahab and his wife, Jezebel were very bad news. Ahab decided he wanted a neighbor's vineyard. So he and Jezebel hatched up a plan that got the neighbor convicted of crime he didn't do and then got him killed for it. Jezebel went on building temples and hiring priests for her false gods and Ahab let her do it when he knew better. Ahab was doing a dog paddle in a cesspool of sin, and he wasn't even trying to keep his head above the surface.

The day Ahab saw God's prophet Elijah standing in front of him, he knew he was in trouble big time. Elijah told Ahab that the Lord said: "I am going to bring disaster on you" (1 Kings 21:21). What kind of disaster? Dogs *will* lap up your blood when you die. And Ahab knew God meant it.

"Ahab tore his clothes, put on sackcloth, and fasted. He lay in sackcloth and went around meekly" (1 Kings 21:27). The guy was a complete wreck! God took pity on the totally remorseful Ahab and told Elijah, "I will not bring this disaster in his day, but I will bring it on his house in the days of his son" (1 Kings 21:28). Ahab was spared. But would you believe it? As soon as he saw he was out of the doghouse, he refused to change any more.

Some More Bad News

King Jehoshaphat of Judah came to see Ahab one day about the little town of Ramoth Gilead that the King of Aram had taken and was still holding. The two kings decided to take the town back. The king of Judah said, "First seek the counsel of the Lord" (1 Kings 22:5). What an interesting idea!

So, Ahab consulted a prophet. The prophet told Ahab that God *did* want him to go to war with Aram. Hey, great! But only so he could *die* in battle.

Really Bad News

King Ahab rode off to war. The king of Aram told his 32 chariot commanders that their ONE mission in the battle was to destroy King Ahab. Ahab took off his kingly robes and disguised himself in regular soldiers' clothes. During the battle, the commanders couldn't find him. But get THIS! An archer randomly shot an arrow and TWHACK! the arrow took Ahab right between the pieces of his armor. Ahab slowly bled to death as he stood watching the battle, and his blood—drip, drip, dripped onto the chariot floor. When he was dead and the battle was over, they washed Ahab's chariot by a river. Dogs came and slurped up his blood, just like Elijah had said.

GET SMARTER

Every evil deed that Ahab did was like a evil seed in his life. Before he knew it, all those evil seeds had grown into thorny vines that cut him off from God and a good life. If he had stopped sinning, God could have cut down those evil thorns. But instead, Ahab harvested a patch of trouble for himself and his family. We can take some gardening tips from old Ahab:

- Live life God's way by planting good seeds that grow into a harvest of God's blessing and love.
- Do the right things now so that you will have a future that is exciting, rewarding, and totally cool. That's how God has things planned!
- Get with the plan!

BIBLE SUPERCHARGE

Do not be deceived: God cannot be mocked. A man reaps what he sows.

Galatians 6:7

ELISHA
[2 KINGS 2-8]

- A real handyman.

- Started out as a farmer.

- Worked for Elijah for a while.

- Asked for twice as much powe[r] as Elijah had.

- Got it.

- Showed tough love to those w[ho] did evil.

- Did tons of miracles.

- Still prophesying when he was dying.

- A corpse brushed against his bones after he died and the person came back to life.

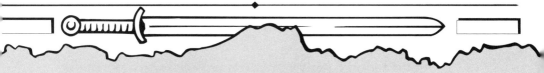
A REALLY GREAT GUY!

He had been plowing his family's field when Elijah called and said to follow him. So Elisha became Elijah's assistant. When Elijah was carried off in the fiery chariot, Elisha took up right where he had left off.

BUNCHES OF MIRACLES

First thing Elisha did was to pick up Elijah's coat and hit the river with it! Immediately the water parted and Elisha walked across the river bottom. Pretty good for miracle number one!

He fixed the city of Jericho's bad water by putting salt in the spring. Never had a problem with that spring again.

One day a widow begged Elisha for help. She was being pressured to sell her sons into slavery to pay off her dead husband's debt. Elisha told her what to do. She obeyed and God gave her so much money she paid off her debts and lived on what was left.

NO PATIENCE WITH TROUBLEMAKERS

The king of Aram had tried to ambush the king of Israel many times, but nothing worked, because Elisha kept warning the king of Israel. In one of his not-so-bright moments the king of Aram decided he'd better sneak up on Elisha and capture him.

So he sent troops to Dothan where Elisha was staying. When Elisha saw the troops, he prayed that the army of Aram would be "blind" to what was really going on. Elisha then told the soldiers that they were in the wrong city. He directed them to the capital city. SURPRISE! There they were surrounded and overpowered by Israel's warriors. ANOTHER SURPRISE! Elisha told the king of Israel to feed the Aramean troops and send them home.

Can you imagine the soldiers trying to explain what had happened to them? The king was astonished and gave up on trying to catch Elisha. Even on his deathbed, Elisha was still helping the king of Israel know how to defeat Aram.

Then Elisha died, but he wasn't through yet. One day, some Israelites were burying a man when raiders came riding up. The frightened people dumped the body into Elisha's tomb and ran off. When the corpse banged into Elisha's bones, the man came back to life. A very cool guy, that Elisha.

BIBLICAL TIMES

GET SMARTER

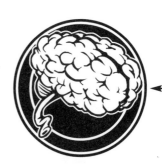

Elisha was God's problem-solver. God still needs those today. Want to be one? Here's how.

- You gotta be dependable. People have to know they can count on you.
- You gotta be listening to hear what God is saying.
- You gotta be willing to start small and grow in serving God.
- You gotta keep saying yes to God.

BIBLE SUPERCHARGE

"Well done, my good servant!" his master replied. "Because you have been trustworthy in a very small matter, take charge of ten cities."

Luke 19:17

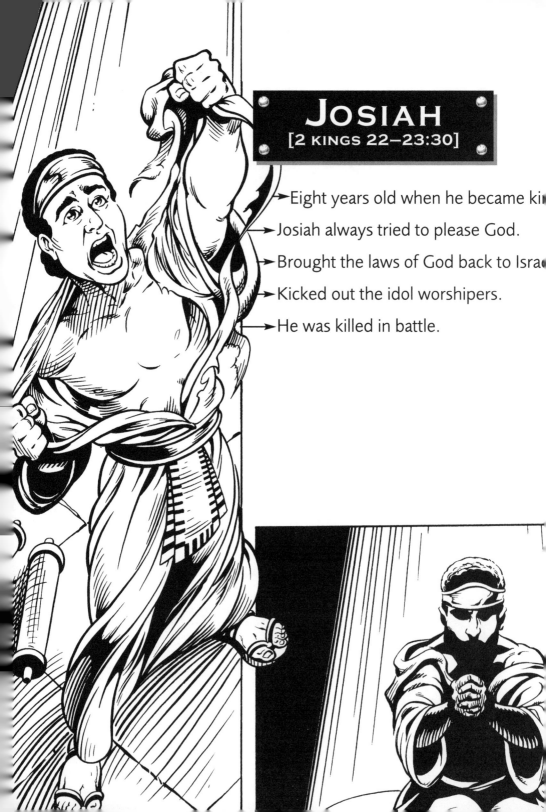

JOSIAH
[2 KINGS 22–23:30]

→ Eight years old when he became ki[ng]

→ Josiah always tried to please God.

→ Brought the laws of God back to Isra[el]

→ Kicked out the idol worshipers.

→ He was killed in battle.

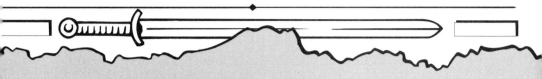

STARTING YOUNG

Prince Josiah was only eight years old when he became king. But he was a smart eight-year-old. He made King David his role model. And like his hero, Josiah always tried to please God. God's temple was badly in need of repair, so one day Josiah gave the order for the temple to be repaired and cleaned out.

Not long after, Hilkiah, the High Priest, found the Book of the Law in the rubble of the Temple. He gave it to Shaphan, the secretary, who read it. Then Shaphan took it to the king and began reading it to King Josiah. It was a super discovery! In the book were all the rules and laws given to Israel by God.

One reading got Josiah so upset he tore his robes (that was the way people used to show extreme sorrow). He realized his people didn't know a thing about God. He decided he had to change all that! The first thing he did was to pray to God for advice, forgiveness, and help.

Next, Josiah gathered the entire kingdom at Solomon's temple. "The king...renewed the covenant in the presence of the Lord–to follow the Lord and keep his commands, regulations and decrees with all his heart and all his soul" (2 Kings 23:3). Then he had all his people do the same. Josiah offered 37,000 sheep and goats and 3,800 cattle as burnt offering to God. How many gallons of blood do you think they spilled? They must have been knee-deep in the stuff.

Then he gave the boot to all the false idols–any evil thing or person was history. He smashed altars, burned temples, and stopped people from sacrificing their children to the god Molech. He got rid of all the pagan priests, mediums, and those who talked to spirits. When he had finished power-cleaning his kingdom, he taught his people about God and his Law.

A TRAGIC LOSS

When Josiah had reigned 31 years, the Egyptians marched north to help Assyria fight the Babylonians. Josiah should have stayed home, but he goofed and took his army out to try to stop Pharaoh. During the battle, Josiah was killed, and he was taken back to Jerusalem where he was buried. Josiah's death was a tragic loss, and the prophet Jeremiah wrote several beautiful and emotional songs in memory of him.

GET DEEPER

Josiah didn't even know there was a book about God. But as soon as he read it, he instantly made changes for himself and for his entire kingdom. He was blown away by what he read in the Bible. Did you know there's some VERY cool stuff in the Bible? We should get excited about what we find in it, and then put that knowledge into action in our lives. God wrote it for us, we read it, and then we live it!

BIBLE SUPERCHARGE

Anyone who listens to the word but does not do what it says is like a man who looks at his face in a mirror and, after looking at himself, goes away and immediately forgets what he looks like.

James 1:23–24

JEREMIAH
[BOOK OF JEREMIAH]

Son of a priest. ◄───

God singled him out ───◄
before he was born.

He became an advisor to kings. ◄───

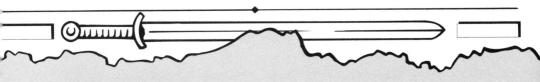
JUST A KID

Jeremiah was a PK–a priest's kid. When he was a teenager, God told him about a very wild job he had reserved just for him. "'Before I formed you in the womb I knew you, before you were born I set you apart; I appointed you as a prophet to the nations'" (Jeremiah 1:5). Jeremiah's jaw hit the floor. Hold on! I'm just a kid! News flash, Jeremiah! God knew your age before he talked to you. God will always be there to save you.

Jeremiah was God's prophet when the big bad Babylonian Empire was trashing kingdoms right, left, and center. Babylon had become filthy rich with the plunder and tribute money they took from weaker kingdoms. Captured slaves also made the kingdom rich as a healthy male slave was worth 20 shekels of silver.

JEREMIAH SAYS "WATCH OUT"

Jeremiah warned Judah that if they didn't get right with God, the Babylonians would attack them and make them slaves. Nobody listened. King Jehoiakim of Judah refused to pay tribute to Nebuchadnezzar, king of Babylon, so Neb attacked Jerusalem, plundered Solomon's temple, and killed Jehoiakim. Nebuchadnezzar took 10,000 of Judah's princes, officers, and important families to Babylon as captives.

Nebuchadnezzar let one of Jehoiakim's sons, Zedekiah, rule Judah under Babylonian control. Jeremiah warned King Zed not to cause trouble with Babylon, BUT ... Zedekiah got together with a few other kings and decided to rebel. Of course, Nebuchadnezzar came back to thrash Judah ONE MORE time. The siege was on, and it would last two years.

Nobody Listens

Inside the city, Jeremiah tried to warn Zedekiah...but nobody likes to hear bad news. Jeremiah was tired of getting picked on for giving God's messages. He wished he had never been born. God told Jeremiah to stop moaning.

Meanwhile, the king's advisors complained that Jeremiah's doom and gloom words were frightening the soldiers. They wanted Jeremiah dead. Zedekiah gave them the okay and had Jeremiah tossed into a mud-filled well and left for dead. Wait a minute, guys! Jeremiah was just telling it like it was! But before Jeremiah sucked up any mud, a powerful black man named Ebed-Melech pulled him back out of the well.

Nebuchadnezzar conquered Jerusalem and killed all the nobles of Judah. Everything Jeremiah had said would happen did happen. For a while Jeremiah stayed in what was left of Judah. But after the Babylonian governor was killed, other rebellious Jews carted Jeremiah off to Egypt. He probably lived in Egypt until his death.

GET COOLER

Jeremiah got to feeling sorry for himself because everybody was mad at HIM, when it was God who was giving him the messages. He felt like God was abusing him. God didn't like that attitude. When we talk to God, we have to remember he is GOD. He doesn't mind us discussing how we feel with him, or hearing questions we might have, but we need to be respectful toward him. You can chat with God—just don't be a brat!

BIBLE SUPERCHARGE

I speak of your faithfulness and salvation. I do not conceal your love and your truth from the great assembly.

Psalm 40:10

SHADRACH, MESCHACH & ABEDNEGO
[DANIEL 3]

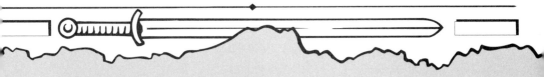
ON FIRE FOR GOD?

Three young guys–Hananiah, Mishael, and Azariah–were dumped into a Babylonian boot camp run by the king of Babylon. Faster than you can say "A-TENNNN-SHUN!" their names were changed to Shadrach, Meschach and Abednego. One day, the king sent them rich food for dinner! Rather than all that fat-inducing food, they asked for a veggie platter.

At first the answer was "No can do." Their overseer worried that they might get weak and sick eating only vegetables. But the boys begged for a trial period. Turned out, they ended up looking even healthier than the rest. Touché! Score one for the Musketeers!

God further blessed these guys with amazing under-standing and wisdom. When the king tested them he found that they were ten times smarter than any Babylonians he had on his staff–which would mean that they had test scores of ... oh ... about 900%.)

Yeah ... but there was one little problem. King Neb got the idea in his head that it would be ultra-cool to build a gianormous golden statue, 9 feet wide and 90 feet tall. This was not just ANY statue, but a giant bow-down-and-worship-or-be-cooked type idol. Some rat was quick to notice that the Three Musketeers weren't bowing, and ratted on them.

King Neb repeated his order: Worship the statue or be hog-tied and chucked into a blazing furnace. The boys just shrugged. "If we are thrown into the blazing furnace, the God we serve is able to save us from it, and he will rescue us from your hand, O king" (Daniel 3:17).

That really got King Neb hot under the crown. He ordered his men to load on the wood and make the furnace seven times hotter than normal. The furnace was so white hot that the flames shooting out made fritters out of the soldiers who threw the three boys in. Hooo-eeee! HOT stuff!

King Neb couldn't believe his royal eyeballs. There were Shadrach, Meschach, and Abednego walking around INSIDE the furnace! They weren't screaming in agony, their skin wasn't burning off, their hair wasn't even singed! But wait! His Neb-ness squinted as he stared inside There was a FOURTH guy in there who looked like a son of the gods! Who was HE and how'd he get in there? Neb shouted for the boys to exit and they strolled on out–not even smelling like smoke. Nebuchadnezzar was astounded! He ordered that no one EVER say a thing against the incomparable God of Shadrach, Meschach, and Abednego. Oh yeah...and he gave them even more powerful jobs running his kingdom.

GET COOLER

Shadrach, Meschach, and Abednego were absolute trendsetters for God. They made a heroic stand. Not only did that please God, but very likely other guys were watching them and then did the same. They made their own lives better, and their good influence on the king resulted in laws being made to protect the rights of Jews to worship God openly and freely. Three Musketeers nothing—they were the Three Meteorites! They made a DEEP IMPACT on the entire empire!

BIBLE SUPERCHARGE

Do not turn away after useless idols. They can do you no good, nor can they rescue you, because they are useless.

1 Samuel 12:21

JOB
[BOOK OF JOB]

- Always faithful to God.

- Became Satan's target.

- Lost everything except his wife and a few friends.

- Was infected with a terrible case of boils.

- Wouldn't give up his faith in God.

- Got more than he ever had before.

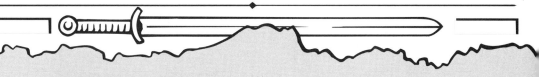

A GREAT GUY

EVERYBODY loved Job! And why not? He had everything. One day Satan was arguing with God about Job. Satan said something like, "Job is a goodie-goodie because you give him EVERYTHING he needs or wants. If you take away Job's good life, he'll turn away from you." God said, "Fine, test your theory. Pull the rug out from under him. But I'm telling you, you're wrong."

TROUBLE HERE

Suddenly Job's good life went down the drain. Here's what happened:

- Job's servants were with his oxen and donkeys when raiders attacked. Only one servant survived to report.
- While Job was listening to that report ANOTHER servant staggered in ... all of Job's shepherds and sheep had been fried by lightning.
- Then a THIRD messenger collapsed in front of Job, moaning that more marauders had

murdered more servants and made off with his camels.

- Then a FOURTH servant rushed through the door to tell Job that all his children had all been killed when their brother's house collapsed in a windstorm.

What a nightmare! Job felt like he'd been punched in the guts. What did he do? He prayed and praised God. And God was pleased with Job's response.

IT GETS WORSE

Then Satan said, "But he still has his health!" "Fine, Devil, do your sickness thing," God answered. Suddenly Job was plastered head to toe by utterly disgusting bad-smelling sores. The poor guy used a broken piece of pottery to scrap pus from his boils. Job was a wreck! His wife told him to curse God, then lie down and die.

Not Job. Not once did he swerve from loving God! Some of Job's "helpful" friends told him that he must have sinned and that God was punishing him. Job knew that wasn't true, but he decided to talk to God to find out why all this was happening to him.

God's answer was simple. Basically God explained that he had his reasons for everything and told Job to have faith that it was all right and good—even if he couldn't understand why. "Job, you can't understand the reasons why I do things. Just hang in there." Sure enough, Job kept his faith in his great God. In the end, Satan was proven wrong. No matter what he did, he couldn't dent Job's relationship with God. After awhile God gave him twice as much as he had before.

GET DEEPER

Always remember: Tough times don't mean that God's against us! Sometimes trouble just happens– and that's okay. Just remember, we can always work through our trouble WITH God's help. God's always there no matter what, and he loves us. We can always trust God to be on our support team one-hundred percent of the time.

BIBLE SUPERCHARGE

Even though I walk through the valley of the shadow of death, I will fear no evil, for you are with me; your rod and your staff, they comfort me.

Psalms 23:4

MARY
[LUKE 1—2]

Young girl.

Lived in Nazareth.

Engaged to Joseph.

Saw an angel.

Became the mother of Jesus.

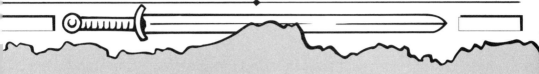

JUST AN ORDINARY GIRL

Mary was just a young girl in a dusty, ho-hum little town called Nazareth, but God had an amazing future for her. One day the angel Gabriel showed up, surprising the socks right off Mary. He said, "Do not be afraid, Mary, you have found favor with God" (Luke 1:30).

What does that mean? "You will be with child and give birth to a son, and you are to give him the name Jesus. He will be great and will be called the Son of the Most High" (Luke 1:31–32).

Now, this was GREAT news. Mary was to be the mother of the Messiah. But you gotta understand, this news created its own set of problems: Mary wasn't married yet. If she became pregnant, people would assume she'd been fooling around. Even Joseph, her husband-to-be, might not believe her. In those days she could have been stoned to death as a result of her announcement. Her response? She blinked a couple times then said, "I am the Lord's servant."

HER SON, JESUS, IS BORN

Sure enough, Joseph did find her explanation hard to swallow. Then an angel came to him in a dream and said, "Mary's child is from the Holy Spirit!" So Joseph married Mary and soon Jesus was born. Many people came to honor the new king, but King Herod (bad guy music please), Israel's rotten ruler, wasn't about to risk losing his throne to a little Jewish baby.

Another angel came to Joseph in his dream and told him to get up and take Mary and the baby to Egypt.

NOW! Off they went in a rush because Herod had ordered his soldiers to murder every baby boy under two years of age in Bethlehem.

After King Herod died, they returned to their home in Nazareth. Mary watched her son grow into an impressive young man of God. Then the day came that he left home and began to travel around Judea and Galilee teaching, performing miracles, and healing the sick.

He did that until the day he was arrested. It was terrifying for Mary to see her son whipped and sentenced to die on a cross. She stood beside his cross and watched helplessly while he died in agony. Jesus looked down at her and told his close friend and disciple, John, to take care of her as he would his own mother. A short while later, he let out a final cry and died. Heartbroken, Mary stood there taking it all in.

NOW SHE UNDERSTOOD

Imagine her complete, total, never-felt-like-THIS-before excitement when she heard that Jesus had risen from the dead! Her son was alive! Then 40 days later Jesus rose up into the clouds and went to be with his Father in heaven. Mary had lost her earthly son but the world had gained a Savior.

GET DEEPER

It's really important to be ready to do what God asks. Mary is a really good example of being ready. She could say "yes" with no strings attached. She didn't wonder, "What's in it for me?" Any ordinary person can become an extraordinary hero if he or she is willing to do God's will.

BIBLE SUPERCHARGE

Teach me to do your will, for you are my God.

Psalms 143:10

HEROD,
THE NOT-SO-GREAT
[MATTHEW 2]

- A really rotten ruler.

- Was an Edomite, who became a Jew and who worked for Rome.

- Was egotistical, evil, violent, selfish, sinful, hateful, and suspicious.

- Built lots of big important stuff.

- Killed babies.

- Died a disgusting death.

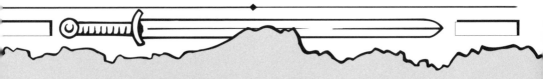
A Rotten Guy

If you made a list of really rotten personality traits and searched the Bible to find someone who matched that list, you'd probably be looking at King Herod the Great. The Roman Empire had taken over Israel. Rome handpicked an Edomite-become-Jew (Herod) for king and told him what to do. He was Rome's puppet.

He Liked to Build Big Stuff to Impress People

Now, most Jews really disliked Herod. He built palaces, forts, a stadium, a theater, and a seaport. Then to try to become popular with the people, he rebuilt God's temple, making it a wonder of the world. "NOW do you like me? Huh? Huh?" Not a chance. Herod was like a guy with knock-you-over-it's-so-bad B.O., who sprinkled a little perfume of "good deeds" in his armpits. It just didn't cut it.

A Suspicious King

Because he was so evil inside, Herod naturally suspected that everybody else was as evil as himself. He was so suspicious of people that he even knocked off his own family members and friends. He thought they were plotting to take his throne, power, and money. Then he heard talk about a new king being born in Bethlehem. His freak-out meter went right off the scale. He ordered his soldiers to Bethlehem to butcher every baby boy under two years of age. They did—but they missed Jesus because an angel had warned Joseph and he had hightailed it to Egypt with Mary and Jesus.

As for Herod, he was a very suspicious, worried, and unhappy guy. He ruled for 37 years and, shortly after Jesus' birth, Herod died of some pretty disgusting and smelly diseases.

Get
Stronger

If you want the real way to be stronger, be a good leader, NOT like Herod who used and bullied everybody in sight. He did whatever he wanted, to get what ever he wanted. Hellloooo! That is NOT the way to live your life. Yet ... you and I ARE sometimes like that in little ways. Have you ever told a friend that you won't hang out with him unless he lets you borrow his bike or whatever? Come ON! Stuff like that is sooo lame. If you want to have good relationships with people, you have be willing to share, be kind, and work together so that everybody has fun hanging out together.

Bible
Supercharge

Watch out! Be on your guard against all kinds of greed; a man's life does not consist in the abundance of his possessions.

Luke 12:15

HEROD ANTIPAS
[MATTHEW 14]

- The nasty son of Herod the Great.

- Got a chunk of his father's kingdom when dad died.

- Had a rotten wife—Herodias.

- Cut off the head of John the Baptist.

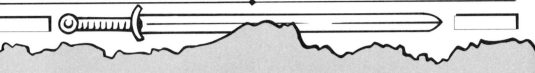
LIKE FATHER, LIKE SON

Herod Antipas, the son of Herod the Great was as rotten as his father. When dad died, Herod A got a chunk of the kingdom.

When John the Baptist was preaching, he had quite a few things to say about Herod Antipas–none of them positive. John told Herod to stop sinning! Did Herod get the message and change his ways? Nope. He just got all pouty and had John thrown in jail.

Truth was, Herod wanted to kill John. But John was incredibly popular and Herod worried that killing John would make the people riot. So John sat in jail. When Herod's birthday came, his wife Herodias threw him a big bash. She even had her slinky daughter dance for Herod. Herod was sooo pleased that he promised to give the girl anything she asked for. Since Herodias hated John with a vengeance, she told her daughter to ask for John's head (you know, without the body.) This really upset Herod, but he'd promised, so he gave the order.

When Jesus was arrested three years later, Pilate sent him to Herod. Herod loved a good show. He wanted to see a miracle. Do a little miracle for me, Jesus. Maybe turn this brick into bread? Jesus wouldn't even talk to him much less do miracles. Well, THIS isn't any

fun! Herod let his soldiers dress Jesus up in royal
robes and mock him. The Roman governor, Pontius
Pilate, thought that was very funny.

Later, when Herod lost a battle with the king of
Aretas, he was exiled to either Spain or France. So
Israel didn't have Herod to kick around anymore.
Herod tried to keep his sins a secret.

GET SMARTER

Guess what? You can't hide a thing from God. Sometimes when we feel guilty about something, we avoid going to church or talking to God. But that doesn't make sin go away. The best thing to do is to go talk to God about it and ask him to help you change your ways or correct the situation. It's the smart thing to do.

BIBLE SUPERCHARGE

Anyone who hides his sins doesn't succeed. But anyone who admits his sins and gives them up finds mercy.

Proverbs 28:13

JESUS
[THE WHOLE BIBLE]

- The Ultimate Bible Hero.
- The Son of God.
- The Son of Mary.
- The One around whom the whole Bible turns.
- The center of history.
- Our Lord and Savior.

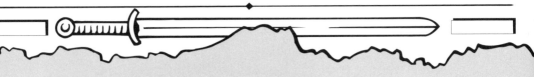

GOOD NEWS FOR THE WHOLE EARTH

Jesus was different! He traveled across his country teaching people about his loving Father in heaven and about what heaven was like. Remember, he had just come from there! He taught about how he was the way to heaven, and he also taught people how to live a good life God's way.

HE LOVED PEOPLE

Lots of people followed Jesus. From them, Jesus picked twelve guys and called them Apostles. These guys stuck to Jesus like a sandal to a foot, and learned everything they could from him. That was just what Jesus wanted. He wanted them to learn everything he had to tell them. He wanted them to pass on to others the things he said and did.

To show people how much God loved them, Jesus healed sick folks, helped the needy, and did mind-boggling miracles. People were in absolute awe of Jesus. They were puzzled too. Everywhere he went, thousands of curious people swarmed around him.

Some Bad News People

Some religious teachers and leaders were very uptight about the things Jesus taught. They didn't like it that some people thought he was the Messiah. They thought Jesus was a deceiver and a troublemaker, so they decided that Jesus had to be killed. It took some doing, but they finally arrested him and had the Romans put him to death.

End of Story? No Way!

Three days after Jesus died, he rose from the dead and appeared to his disciples. They were shocked. They were stunned. But it was true. For the next 40 days Jesus laid out his plan for them. They were to tell the world the GOOD NEWS about Jesus! Then he went to be with his Father in heaven. Last, but not least, he said he was coming back to earth at the end of this age.

Questions and Answers

When on earth, Jesus lived just like us ordinary people. Except for one thing: He never did anything sinful or bad and he always, always obeyed God.

Q: So why did Jesus come to earth?
WE sin and disobey God and need a Savior.
Q: Will God's love ever stop?
Never! Jesus and his Father will always love us.
Q: How do we get to heaven?
Jesus is the bridge between his Father in heaven and us. Jesus took the punishment for our sins.

Jesus was nailed to the cross like a common criminal. You gotta know that Jesus loved us a lot to go through THAT for us! He died so our sins could be forgiven and we could become God's children again—and live forever with him.

GET SMARTER, STRONGER, DEEPER & COOLER

Absolutely ANYbody in the world can choose to follow Jesus anytime. That's why he came to earth. Choose Jesus and he rescues you from the slime pit of sin. That makes Jesus the biggest hero who ever was, is, and will ever be. When we follow his example in everything, we will become the best we can be.

BIBLE SUPERCHARGE

And Jesus grew in wisdom and stature, and in favor with God and men.

Luke 2:52

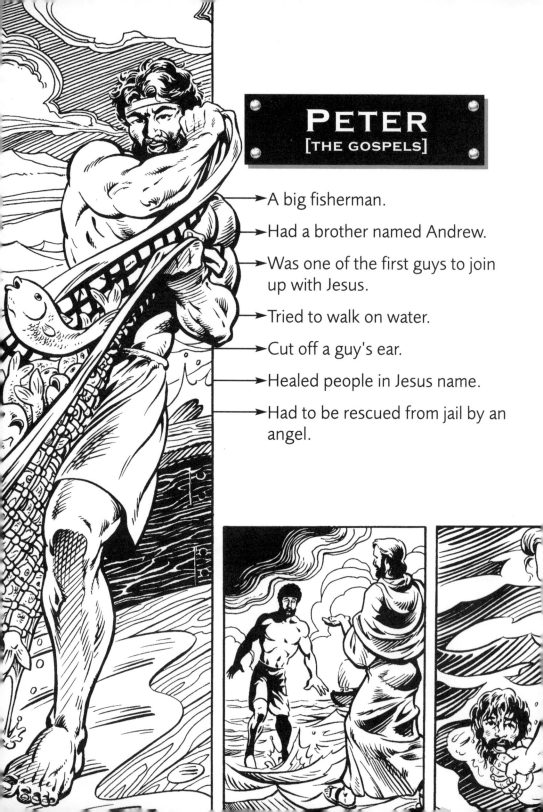

PETER
[THE GOSPELS]

- A big fisherman.
- Had a brother named Andrew.
- Was one of the first guys to join up with Jesus.
- Tried to walk on water.
- Cut off a guy's ear.
- Healed people in Jesus name.
- Had to be rescued from jail by an angel.

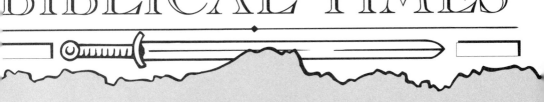

THE ROCK MEETS THE SAVIOR

One day Peter's brother, Andrew, came running to him. He said he had found the Savior, the Messiah! Peter followed Andy to meet Jesus. That day changed Peter's life forever! Jesus gave him a new name—"The Rock." Peter stayed close to Jesus and learned all he could from him.

Peter made plenty of dumb mistakes, but he didn't give up. Here are some of the things he did:

Walked on water. One day Jesus sent his disciples across a lake in a boat. During the night an incredible storm hit. Peter spotted Jesus walking as calmly as you please through the rain and darkness on the dark, wild water right toward them! So Peter got out of the boat to walk to Jesus on the water too. But before he got all the way to Jesus, he lost his nerve, and BLOOOP! down he went.

Said the right thing at the right time. The crowds believed that Jesus was really John the Baptist or the prophet Elijah come back to life. When Jesus asked his disciples who they thought he was, Peter said, "You are the Son of God." And Peter was right.

Said the wrong thing at the right time. Later when Jesus told his disciples that he would be killed,

Peter argued, "No way!" Then Jesus spoke sharply to Peter: "You are a stumbling block to me; you don't have in mind the things of God, but the things of man" (Matthew 16:23).

Sliced off a guy's ear. When the soldiers came to arrest Jesus, Peter whipped out a sword and sliced off a guy's ear.

Denied he knew Jesus. Jesus was arrested and Peter was so scared of being caught he told a servant girl he didn't even know Jesus. Later Peter was so ashamed of what he'd done that he bawled his eyes out for hours.

Chatted with Jesus after the resurrection. After Jesus came back to life, he had a personal chat with Peter to let him know he was forgiven.

Preached to thousands. Jesus went back to heaven and Peter, filled with the Holy Spirit, and courage belted out the first open-air sermon of the Christian church.

The rest of the story. For the next few years, Peter went on to bravely teach about Jesus and to heal people. He was arrested, flogged, thrown in jail, and run out of town. But he just would NOT stop talking about Jesus. He took the message to Jews first, and then to the Gentiles.

Many people believe Peter was crucified in Rome when

Nero was persecuting and killing the early Christians. That's probably what happened. But Peter was ready to die for Jesus!

GET SMARTER

Peter was an unschooled country hick with a thick clumsy country way of speaking. That's what the world saw. What Jesus saw in Peter was a brave, loving, standup, rock-solid kind of guy. God sees you not only for who you are, but who you WILL be in the future. Even though Peter made mistakes, Jesus knew he was just the man for the job. Peter was a work in progress. We ALL are! Let God work in you and change your heart day by day. That's how heroes are made!

BIBLE SUPERCHARGE

When they saw the courage of Peter and John and realized that they were unschooled, ordinary men, they were astonished and they took note that these men had been with Jesus.

Acts 4:13

JUDAS ISCARIOT
[MARK 14]

A traitor.

One of the twelve disciples.

Carried the money bag for the group.

Betrayed Jesus to the religious leaders.

Later, hung himself.

THE BAD APPLE IN THE BARREL

Judas Iscariot was one of Jesus' disciples but man oh man, he sure wasn't a friend! He traveled with Jesus, watching him teach, heal the sick, and do miracles. But somehow the lights just weren't going on in Judas' attic. He didn't get this Messiah idea.

Judas was in charge of the money that was given to Jesus' band of travelers. He was greedy for money. One evening while Jesus was having dinner with a friend, a woman poured expensive perfume on him. Judas grumbled that the perfume could have been sold for a year's wages and the money given to the poor. Of course, the "poor" he had in mind was himself.

THE GREAT BETRAYAL

After the perfume event, Judas decided to hand Jesus over to the Jewish religious leaders who hated him. When one of the religious leaders waved 30 pieces of silver under his nose to betray his Master, greedy Judas grabbed it.

We don't fully know what his motives were. We do know that Satan fed on his greed, anger, and doubt.

John says that "Satan entered into him" (John 13:27) when he betrayed Jesus. The priests were thrilled! Judas agreed to help them arrest Jesus when he was away from the crowds. Jesus already knew that Judas was going to betray him, and during his last meal with his disciples, he told Judas to get it done and over with. Judas took off to do his wicked deed.

That night, Jesus and his disciples were praying in a garden called Gethsemane, when Judas showed up. He walked out of the shadows, puckered up his lips, and planted a big old kiss on Jesus' cheek. Yuck! That kiss was the sign to the soldiers that this was the man they wanted.

GUILTY!

The soldiers rushed into the garden and captured Jesus. Judas had done his job.

But a little later when Judas learned that Jesus had been beaten, whipped, and was about to be crucified, he became desperate with guilt. He rushed back to the chief priests and tried to return their money, blubbering that he had helped kill an innocent man.

Huh! Did they care? Not at all, and they weren't giving Jesus back. So Judas stumbled out, found a rope, and hung himself. Later when his corpse was cut down or fell, his body burst open and his intestines slopped out all over the ground. His evil actions had brought him to a really messy, utterly gross end!

GET DEEPER

Judas' sinful actions may have started out small at first, but over time, little sins became a habit. Then years later he's tying a rope to a branch and wondering, "How did I get here?" Sin is like taking little bites at a piece of tasty bait on a fishhook. SUDDENLY we've got a chunk of metal sticking through our jaw and we're being reeled in to someplace we do NOT want to go.

The way to avoid sin is to avoid that bait in the first place. But if sin DOES catch us, we have to call up Jesus' catch-and-release program. Only Jesus can get us off the hook and help us change our ways.

BIBLE SUPERCHARGE

So turn away from your sins. Turn to God. Then your sins will be wiped away.

Acts 3:19

PONTIUS PILATE
[MARK 15]

- Roman ruler in Jerusalem.

- Hated Jews.

- Didn't see what the big fuss was about Jesus.

- Tried to bargain with the crowd

- Had Jesus beaten to try to get him freed.

- Didn't listen to his wife when she warned him.

- Gave up and crucified Jesus.

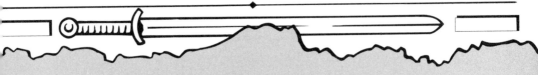
A REAL TOUGH-GUY

Rome ruled Israel and the Roman in charge of keeping Israel under control was Pontius Pilate. Here was a man who did NOT like Jews. Once, after putting a number of Jews to death, he mixed their blood with the blood of the animals they had sacrificed. Charming.

WHAT'S THE PROBLEM?

Pilate was unimpressed when the Jewish leaders first brought a minor troublemaker named Jesus to his office. Big deal. Case dismissed. Next!

But the religious leaders were really over-the-top upset this time. But Pilate couldn't find any reason in Roman law to charge him. Plus ... there was something about this quiet man that Pilate didn't understand. Pilate sent Jesus to see King Herod because Jesus was from Herod's territory, Galilee. Herod sent Jesus right back. Pilate's gut instincts told him Jesus was innocent. So what should he do?

TRYING TO BARGAIN

Wait! There was a solution. He'd bargain with the crowd by asking them if they wanted a terrible criminal released or Jesus, the man he believed innocent. About that time his wife sent him a note. She'd had a bad dream about Jesus and urged her husband to have nothing to do with him. Well, then Pilate asked the Jews who they wanted him to release to them. Jesus? Or the filthy, despicable murderer named Barabbas? The answer roared back from the crowd. "Give us Barabbas! Crucify Jesus!"

Pilate knew this wasn't right. Maybe if they saw a little blood it would satisfy them. So he had Jesus whipped and beaten. Did that work? Nope. The religious leaders wanted Jesus dead.

Jesus wasn't helping matters by staying so quiet. When Pilate asked, "Don't you know I have the power to crucify you?" Jesus answered that the only power Pilate had came from God. Now Pilate was completely shook up, and the mob outside his porch was nearly out of control.

Pilate had a bowl of water brought to him. He washed his hands in front of the angry crowd. "'I am innocent of this man's blood,' he said. 'It is your responsibility!'" (Matthew 27:24). Pilate then ordered Jesus executed, but, he just did NOT have a good feeling about this.

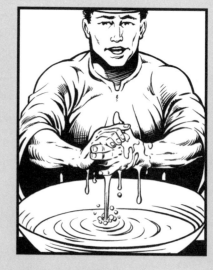

It took time, but all Pilate's years of political bungling finally caught up with him and he was sent packing, jobless, to some cold part of the Roman Empire. Some say he killed himself.

GET SMARTER

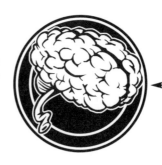

Pilate was a nasty, ungodly ruler, but he was stopped cold by Jesus. He was also weak and didn't do what he knew was right.

- He knew he should free Jesus because he was innocent.
- He was afraid of what Caesar might say and do to him if the religious leaders went to the ruler in Rome.
- He was trapped in the role of the Roman governor.
- Doing right and allowing wrong were all mixed up in his mind.

Sometimes if WE'RE not careful, we can split up our life too. One part goes to church and does all the right Christian things, another part forgets being a Christian and acts differently. Being a Christian is for EVERY part of our lives and for all the time in our life. It's an all the time thing.

BIBLE SUPERCHARGE

Watch your life and doctrine closely. Persevere in them, because if you do, you will save both yourself and your hearers.

1 Timothy 4:16

STEPHEN
[ACTS 6–7]

- Loved helping other people.

- A real go-getter-for-God guy.

- Jewish religious leaders hated him.

- Was executed by the religious leaders.

- Saw Jesus before he went to heaven.

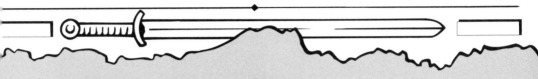

A Really Neat Guy!

Stephen loved working for the church in Jerusalem.
He was a real go-getter, on-fire-for-God kind of guy.
He helped with the day-to-day running of the church.
But Stephen was a guy run plumb off his feet! There
were so many widows and their families to feed.
There were donations to distribute and errands for
elders. Oh, and he also preached and taught. But it
was okay because God blessed Stephen's ministry
with miracles and other great stuff.

Sometimes You Can't Win

Everybody liked him ... except maybe the Jewish religious leaders who were frustrated with him and
spread lies about him. "We have heard Stephen speak
words of blasphemy against Moses and against God"
(Acts 6:11).

NOT TRUE. But true or not, it was enough to get
Stephen arrested and dragged in front of an angry
religious court. God was with Stephen, and the Holy
Spirit gave him the right words to speak. Stephen was
bold and filled with God's power.

The people in the court saw Stephen's face glowing
like an angel's face, even as he told the leaders exactly

what he thought! He said they were the ones disobeying God's laws, not him. He told them point blank that they had killed the Son of God.

Oh Oh!

Were the leaders mad? Hoo-eeeee! They SURE were! They ground their teeth so hard they probably chipped the enamel. While they were utterly losing it, Stephen saw heaven open up and Jesus standing beside his Father. "Look," he said, "I see heaven open and the Son of Man standing at the right hand of God" (Acts 7:55).

They went TOTALLY ballistic! They started yelling at the top of their voices while covering their ears so they couldn't hear him. They grabbed Stephen, dragged him outside, picked up stones, and started throwing. While they were killing him, Stephen prayed and asked God to forgive them. You try to beat that!

GET COOLER

We have to forgive others if we want God to forgive us when we blow it. Not forgiving–holding grudges and ignoring people on purpose–is never the right or cool thing to do. Ditch those attitudes. Stephen forgave his killers even while the stones were slamming into his head and ribs. He forgave them even though they didn't ask for or even want forgiveness! That is so absolutely cool.

BIBLE SUPERCHARGE

For if you forgive men when they sin against you, your heavenly Father will also forgive you.

Matthew 6:14

SAUL/PAUL
[ACTS 9–28]

→ A Jew who was also a Roman citizen.

→ Hated Christians.

→ Held the coats when Stephen was stoned.

→ Got knocked off his feet by a vision of Christ.

→ Got changed from the inside out.

→ Got a new name, "Paul".

→ Became one of the apostles of the church.

→ Was a tentmaker, preacher, and teacher.

→ Died as a prisoner of Rome.

ONE MEAN GUY

Saul (Paul) was a Jew who was raised in a wealthy Roman city. This made him a Roman citizen, and that had definite perks! Saul started out as a tentmaker. What he really wanted to be was a Rabbi or religious teacher. It didn't take very long for the religious leaders to notice him. They called on Saul to help stamp out those dangerous Christians.

Saul took on the job of arresting and beating Christians. This suited him just fine because he didn't believe Jesus was God's son, and he hated Christians. One day Saul was on the road to Damascus to do some Christian head-bashing when something happened. A flash of bright light threw Paul to the ground and blinded him. A voice out of nowhere asked, "Why are you persecuting me?" (Acts 9:4). When Saul asked wh-wh-WHO was speaking, the voice replied, "I am Jesus" (Acts 9:6).

A NEW IDENTITY

When Saul could see again, he was a CHANGED man and he got a new name—

Paul! Now he was for Jesus even more than he had been against him. Paul became one of the most unstoppable preachers in the early church. The guy was a walking, talking, preaching machine! He traveled over land and sea, fields and fountains, moor and mountains, preaching everywhere he went. Sometimes he'd perform healings or do miracles. Many people became believers, but just as often, angry religious leaders gave Paul a painful exit out of town. It didn't matter how many times people threw stones at him, arrested him, or even tried to kill him, Paul just kept on talking about Jesus. His enthusiasm started new churches all over the Roman Empire.

LIFE WASN'T EASY

After he became a Christian, Paul had some really tough stuff happen to him. Here's some of it.

- Was almost murdered by an angry mob in Jerusalem.
- Was first rescued, then arrested, by a Roman commander, and was held prisoner for two years.
- Was taken to Rome where he was under house arrest. He continued to teach, preach, and write letters to the churches he had helped start.
- Was released for a short time and went wild preaching again. Soon the Roman Emperor, Nero, gathered up Christian men, women, and children and had them killed in terrible ways in the great Colosseum of Rome.
- Was arrested again on Nero's orders and was put to death because he was a Christian.

GET STRONGER

God doesn't want us to have a so-so attitude about the church. We should have a passionate go-for-it attitude about our faith. Paul went into hyper-speed to spread the good news as far as he could get. So the next time we're asked to get involved at church or school, let's go for it totally with high-energy enthusiasm.

BIBLE SUPERCHARGE

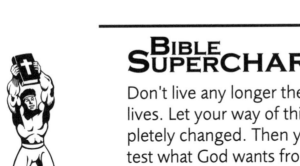

Don't live any longer the way this world lives. Let your way of thinking be completely changed. Then you will be able to test what God wants from you. And you will agree that what He wants is right.

Romans 12:2

2:52 Soul Gear™ books—
Action, adventure, and mystery that only a boy could appreciate!

Available now at your local bookstore!

Laptop 1: Reality Shift
They Changed the Future
Written by Christopher P. N. Maselli
Softcover 0-310-70338-7

Bible Heroes & Bad Guys
Written by Rick Osborne
Softcover 0-310-70322-0

Laptop 2: Double-Take
Things are Not What They Seem
Written by Christopher P. N. Maselli
Softcover 0-310-70339-5

Bible Wars & Weapons
Written by Rick Osborne
Softcover 0-310-70323-9

Look for more great books coming spring 2003

Weird & Gross Bible Stuff
Written by Rick Osborne
Softcover 0-310-70484-7

Laptop 3: Explosive Secrets
*Not Everything Lost
is Meant to be Found*
Written by Christopher P. N. Maselli
Softcover 0-310-70340-9

Bible Fortress, Temples, & Tombs
Written by Rick Osborne
Softcover 0-310-70483-9

Laptop 4: Power Play
Beware of Broken Promises
Written by Christopher P. N. Maselli
Softcover 0-310-70341-7

Zonderkidz™

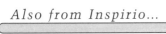

We want to hear from you. Please send your comments
about this book to us in care of the address below.
Thank you.

Zonder**kidz**™

Grand Rapids, MI 49530
www.zonderkidz.com